Kaushik Deb, Anjali Garg, Kai Rommel

Energy Management for the Emerging Megacity Hyderabad

Studying demand, supply and gaps and exploring technical, social and institutional factors

Emerging megacities
Dicussion Papers
Edited by Konrad Hagedorn, Christine Werthmann, Dimitrios Zikos, Ramesh Chennamaneni

Humboldt-Universität zu Berlin
Department of Agricultural Economics
Division of Resource Economics
Philippstr. 13, House 12
10115 Berlin

Tel.: +49 (0)30 2093 6305
Fax: +49 (0)30 2093 6497
www.agrar.hu-berlin.de/struktur/institute/wisola/fg/ress
www.sustainable-hyderabad.de

Contact: emerging.megacities@hu-berlin.de

The emerging megacities discussion papers are available at:
www.eh-verlag.de

ISSN print edition 2193-6927

Emerging megacities Discussion Papers are prepared by researchers working on topics in the realm of sustainable development in Megacities of Tomorrow, a research priority by the German Ministry of Education and Research (BMBF). The papers have been peer-reviewed by a board of external reviewers.
Views and opinions expressed do not necessarily represent those of the Division of Resource Economics.
Comments are highly welcome and should be sent directly to the authors.
We welcome contributions on any topics related to Megacities of Tomorrow. Further information on the submission procedure is given at:
www.sustainable-hyderabad.de/emerging-megacities

Deb, Kaushik; Garg, Anjali; Rommel, Kai

Energy Management for the Emerging Megacity Hyderabad
Studying demand, supply and gaps and exploring technical, social and institutional factors

Emerging megacities Discussion Papers, Volume 3/2009

ISBN/EAN: 978-3-86741-815-7

First published in 2012 by Europaeischer Hochschulverlag GmbH & Co KG, Bremen, Germany.

© Europaeischer Hochschulverlag GmbH & Co KG, Fahrenheitstr. 1, D-28359 Bremen (www.eh-verlag.de). All rights reserved.

Cover: Photo "Metropolis", ferendus (flickr). Creative Commons License

No part of this publication may be reproduced or transmitted, in any form or by any means, electronic, mechanical, photocopying, recording or otherwise, or stored in any retrieval system of nay nature, without the written permission of the copyright holder and the publisher, application for which shall be made to the publisher.

EHV

Energy Management for the Emerging Megacity Hyderabad

Studying demand, supply and gaps and exploring technical, social and institutional factors

Kaushik Deb[*], *Anjali Garg*[*], *Kai Rommel*[†‡]

May 2009

Abstract

The background study represents the first part of the deliverables of the Work Package 3.2. A for milestone one. It reflects the status of the power sector of Andhra Pradesh with specific consideration of Greater Hyderabad. Beside transport, electricity is the main application of energy sources in the areas of generation, transmission, generation and consumption. The study places particular attention, first, to the regulatory framework of the Andhra Pradesh power sector and the linkages to Hyderabad and, second, to the state of the sub-sectors. Based on this we identify sources for inefficient energy use and provide the basis for further analysis of consumption patterns of households and firms in the public and private sectors. The predominant problems of the power sector highlighted in the background study are huge supply gaps and growing peak deficits due to economic growth, insufficient incentives for energy saving investments and limited capacity expansions, because tariff structures fail to set price signals for energy saving measures and application of low emission technologies. The results of the background study indicate several reasons for inefficiencies and supply gaps arising from institutional, economic and technical issues, such as subsidies for irrigation and agriculture failing to set incentives for energy savings for farmers. The background study forms the basis for analysis of strategies to improve energy efficiency and to develop strategies and projects together with the stakeholder analysis in the entire energy sector.

Key words: *background study, energy management, demand, supply, technology, institutions, Hyderabad, India*

---

[*] The Energy and Resource Institute (TERI), Lodhi Road, New Delhi
[†] Corresponding author. Tel.: +49 30 2093 6305. Email: kai.rommel@ism.de
[‡] Division of Resource Economics, Humboldt Universität zu Berlin, Philippstraße 13, 10099 Berlin

1 Introduction

The main objective of the background study is to identify inefficiencies in the energy sector and to reveal the various reasons for supply gaps, high emissions and high losses in transmission and distribution. Based on this, schemes for the implementation of energy saving measures and for cost minimised market regulation are developed. In accordance with the consortium's project schedule, the background study to WP 3.2 A is subdivided into two parts. The first part represents the deliverable for the first milestone by May 2009 and describes the features of the energy sector including generation, transmission, distribution, and consumption. Energy regulation is under the authority of GoAP, therefore energy market analysis of Hyderabad takes into consideration the regulatory framework of AP. For data review we consult the relevant literature on market and regulation analysis and consider information provided by the relevant stakeholders, "APGENCO", "APTRANSCO", "IPP´s", "NEDCAP", "DISCOM", especially the "AP Central Power Distribution Comp. Ltd." (APCPDCL) and the "Energy Conservation Mission" (ECM). Assessment of failures and sufficient efficiency improvements in the energy sector is based on information gained from expert interviews with the stakeholders conducted in February and March 2009. The first part of the background study gives detailed information about failures and shortcomings within the energy sector and, therefore, reduces the complexity of efficiency issues in the energy sector.

Building on the first part, which is mainly descriptive, the second part of the background study is scheduled for the second milestone in 2010 and will provide dynamic sector analysis of production and consumption patterns based on explorative analysis of consumer and producer behaviour. Chapter 4.3 of the background study gives a detailed description of the methodology used in order to generate reliable expert knowledge on individual preferences concerning energy savings and mitigation technology and, in addition, a more clear-cut picture of the various determinants of consumer and firm behaviour.

Both parts of the background study yield a reference scenario of the energy market in Hyderabad, which is embedded in an analysis of the energy sector of Andhra Pradesh and scheduled for milestone two. The reference scenario comprises, first, descriptive elements regarding the energy sector and developments during the last decade. Second, the background study provides an analysis of production and consumption patterns using econometric models in order to identify efficiency optimised paths for further modelling scheduled for the period after the second milestone. Furthermore, the reference scenario illustrates drivers of and obstacles to efficient generation, transmission, distribution, and consumption of electricity and heat. Finally, this knowledge is fundamental for the development and implementation of demonstration projects in order to reduce complexity and to show how to apply energy efficiency measures and policies in households and firms related to adaptation and mitigation of climate change.

After the introduction the presented background study continues with a synthesis of the background study and the stakeholder analysis in Chapter 2. Chapter 3 pictures the regulatory framework in Andhra Pradesh with specific consideration of regulation, market structure, and price developments in Hyderabad. The structure of generation, transmission, distribution, and consumption is the subject of Chapter 4, including an outlook on market behaviour analysis. Chapter 5 summarises required changes and the current plans of stakeholders in terms of efficiency improvements in the energy sector of Andhra Pradesh and Hyderabad. In Chapter 6 we draw some conclusions followed by an outlook on further analysis in the second part of the background study. Detailed data on the energy sector are listed in the annex.

2 Synthesis of the background study and the stakeholder analysis

The deliverable of the WP 3.2 A comprises the background study and the stakeholder analysis. The background study of the energy sector of Andhra Pradesh pictures the detailed structure of the state energy sector and places particular attention on the areas of electricity generation, transmission, and distribution. The stakeholder analysis provides data on the actors in the energy market of Andhra Pradesh and Hyderabad regarding their objectives and interests, organisational structure, incentives, power and resources, and their relation to other stakeholders as well as towards the project's objectives. Stakeholder mapping, the analysis of stakeholder relationships, and the comparison of power and interests regarding the project objectives serve to identify the relevance of stakeholders for project implementation. Stakeholder capacities are considered with project objectives for pilot projects, capacity building, and the planning processes of the Urban Energy Management Plan (UEM) and the Energy Master Plan (EMP) to create the most suitable "winning coalitions" for mitigation and adaptation strategies. The stakeholder analysis plays a significant role for identification of rural-urban linkages in the energy sector. Energy use from generation to consumption serves as cross-cutting issue because access to electricity and other energy sources affects virtually all economic and social areas. Therefore, degree of energy efficiency affects local and social groups in different ways. For example, power cuts are treated different between rural and urban areas. This often affects rural firms stronger compared to other firms, i.e. income effects of power cuts differ between rural and urban areas.

The background study and the stakeholder analysis take these issues into consideration and provide the basis for further analysis and scenario building measures in the energy sector regarding institutional changes towards sustainable efficiency improvements.

3 Regulatory framework, market structure and prices

In 1998 India has passed an electricity reform with the Electricity Regulatory Commissions Act followed by the Electricity Act 2003. The entire reform comprises unbundling of the energy sector and establishment of an independent regulator, the AP Electricity Regulatory Commission (APERC) which was set up by the Government of Andhra Pradesh under the Electricity Regulatory Commissions Act.[1] Since the reform the energy sector is divided into the fields of generation, transmission and distribution. The energy market of Andhra Pradesh is characterised by growing demand surplus due to economic growth and increasing electrification. The following chapter provides a description of the market structure in terms of its size, participants, regulatory framework and instruments, effects of market regulation, deficits of utilisation, and future developments and perspectives.

3.1 Regulatory framework

The APERC was established in 1999 under the provisions of the Andhra Pradesh Electricity Reform (APER) Act 1998. APERC derives its power to grant licenses for transmission and supply of electricity in the State of Andhra Pradesh through Section 15 of the A.P. Electricity Reform Act, 1998.

In February 1999, the APSEB was unbundled into APGENCO and APTRANSCO. While APGENCO was mandated to acquire, establish, construct, and operate power-generating stations in the state, APTRANSCO was made responsible both for transmission & bulk supply and for distribution and retail supply. In March 2000, in accordance to the provisions of the APER Act, the Commission granted approval to APTRANSCO to transfer its distribution and retail supply business to four state-owned DISCOMs. The

---

[1] Shukla et al., 2004: 11 and Lamb, 2006: 40.

Commission issued licenses to APTRANSCO in January 2000 and to the four DISCOMs in December 2000 forming the following distribution and retail supply licensees:

1. **Northern Power Distribution Company of Andhra Pradesh Limited (APNPDCL)** - To cater to the districts of Warangal, Karminar, Khammam, Nizamabad and Adilabad

2. **Eastern Power Distribution Company of Andhra Pradesh Limited (APEPDCL)** - To cater to the operation circles of Srikakulam, Visakhapatnam, Vizianagaram, East and West Godavari districts and 17 Divisions of coastal Andhra Pradesh

3. **Central Power Distribution Company of Andhra Pradesh Limited (APCPDCL)** - To cater to the districts of Anantapur, Kurnool, Mahaboobnagar, Nalgonda, Medak and Rangareddy

4. **Southern Power Distribution Company of Andhra Pradesh Limited (APSPDCL)** - To cater to the districts of Krishna, Guntur, Pakasam, Nellore, Chittoor and Kapada

    The city of Hyderabad comes under the jurisdiction of the APCPDCL.

APERC also awarded licenses to nine Rural Electric Cooperative Societies (RESCOs) operating in the state. Subsequently, the Electricity Act (hereinafter EA 03 or the Act) was notified in June 2003. Even though the Act replaced three existing central legislations, Section 185 (1) clearly mentions that provisions of state Reform Acts (including APER Act 1998) not inconsistent with provisions of the Act shall remain in force. Therefore, the APERC continues to be guided by the provisions of the A.P. Reform Act.

3.2 Functions of APERC

As per Section 86 of the EA 03, the functions of APERC are as follows:

1. The State Commission shall discharge the following functions, namely:

    a) determine the tariff for generation, supply, transmission and wheeling of electricity, wholesale, bulk or retail, as the case may be, within the State:

    Providing that where open access has been permitted to a category of consumers under section 42, the State Commission shall determine only the wheeling charges and surcharge thereon, if any, for the said category of consumers,

b) regulate electricity purchase and procurement process of distribution licensees including the price at which electricity shall be procured from the generating companies or licensees or from other sources through agreements for purchase of power for distribution and supply within the State,

c) facilitate intra-state transmission and wheeling of electricity,

d) issue licenses to persons seeking to act as transmission licensees, distribution licensees and electricity traders with respect to their operations within the State,

e) promote co-generation and generation of electricity from renewable sources of energy by providing suitable measures for connectivity with the grid and sale of electricity to any person, and also specify, for purchase of electricity from such sources, a percentage of the total consumption of electricity in the area of a distribution license,

f) adjudicate upon the disputes between the licensees, and generating companies and to refer any dispute for arbitration,

g) levy fee for the purposes of this Act,

h) specify State Grid Code consistent with the Grid Code specified under clause (h) of sub-section (1) of section 79,

i) specify or enforce standards with respect to quality, continuity and reliability of service by licensees,

j) fix the trading margin in the intra-State trading of electricity, if considered, necessary; and

k) discharge such other functions as may be assigned to it under this Act.

2. The State Commission shall advise the State Government on all or any of the following matters, namely:

   i) promotion of competition, efficiency and economy in activities of the electricity industry,

   ii) promotion of investment in electricity industry,

   iii) reorganisation and restructuring of electricity industry in the State,

   iv) matters concerning generation, transmission, distribution and trading of electricity or any other matter referred to the State Commission by that Government.

3. The State Commission shall ensure transparency while exercising its powers and discharging its functions.
4. In discharge of its functions the State Commission shall be guided by the National Electricity Policy, National Electricity Plan and tariff policy published under section 3.

3.3 Approaches adopted by APERC

Consequent to the enactment of the EA 03, the Commission has issued several important orders; and has formulated and notified a number of regulations on important aspects of supply of electricity to the consumers. These are discussed below:

3.3.1 Approach to tariff determination

Since its first tariff order in 2000–01, APERC has used the Cost-of-Service (CoS) model as the basis for structure and design of retail tariffs for all the DISCOMs in the state. This model is primarily based on the principle of recovering the Commission approved embedded costs by way of tariff adjustments. Other objectives of this tariff model are to identify the extent of cross subsidy and to provide a measure of value for energy saving. Under this model, the Commission initially allocates each cost item (approved) into three headings i.e. energy component, demand component and customer service component. While the energy component comprises of the variable portion of total power purchase costs, the demand component comprises of the fixed portion along with a part of the network costs. The customer service component (i.e. metering, billing and consumer servicing) forms the remaining portion of the network costs. Such classified cost components are apportioned among consumer categories so as to determine the Fully Allocated Costs (FAC). Subsequently, APERC determines the constraints on increase of tariffs in respect of the subsidising categories. The tariff increase in these categories up to the constraint level provides the level of cross-subsidy. Thereafter, the Commission communicates to the Government of Andhra Pradesh (GoAP) enquiring whether the later intends to extend cross-subsidy to a customer category. Based on the government's response, the FAC is assigned to each consumer category and the cost to serve per unit of a category is determined. The later is also referred to as the Fully Allocated Cost Tariff (FACT).

From 2006–07 onwards, however, the Commission, decided to go in for a multi-year tariff framework and accordingly notified the APERC Regulation, 2005 (Terms and

Conditions for Determination of Tariff for Wheeling and Retail Sale of Electricity) in November 2005. Under this Regulation, each distribution licensee has to make the filings as hitherto fore, but in respect of the distribution business, for a control period, generally of 5 years, the first control period, however, being of a 3-year duration (2006–07 to 2008–09). The filings for the retail supply business shall, however, be on annual basis, for the first control period and thereafter for the entire control period for the subsequent control periods. Accordingly, the Commission issued its order on distribution tariffs for the first control period (2006–07 to 2008–09) and the retail supply tariffs for 2006–07 in March 2006. Subsequently, it issued the tariff order for retail supply business of the four distribution companies for 2007–08 in March 2007.

While designing the tariffs for various categories, the Commission has designed tariff to ensure that there is gradual movement of tariffs to align with the cost of supply and towards simplifying the slab structure by reducing the number of slabs in the category. It also incentivised industrial consumers to move from captive consumption to grid supply through mechanisms like load factor rebate (providing discount on energy charge for maintenance of higher load factor).

The APERC has been contemplating introducing time-of-day (ToD) tariffs since 2003–04. Towards this end, the Commission directed the DISCOMs to explore and identify consumers who are using high quantum of electricity and cases where ToD tariffs can be implemented effectively. In tariff order 2004–05, the Commission directed the DISCOMs to specify the following details on metering facility, consumption patterns and proposed incentive for large consumers. However, as per the tariff order 2005–06, the Commission noted that limited progress had been made in specifying a plan for introducing ToD tariffs in the state. Thereafter, the DISCOMs also undertook a study on introducing ToD tariffs in the state. It was observed that the load curve in Andhra Pradesh is flat on account of supply of electricity to agriculture during off-peak period. Moreover, the study revealed that there exist seasonal peaks rather than ToD peaks. Based on this analysis, the Commission has directed the DISCOMs to further investigate into the possibilities of introducing ToD tariff in the state.

3.3.2 Private sector participation and competition

The Commission has also attempted to facilitate competition in state power sector by notifying regulations on terms and conditions of open access (OA) (u/s 42) and trading in electricity (u/s 52). The regulation on 'open access to intra-state transmission and distribution networks' was issued by the APERC in July 2005. The regulation specified the following phasing of open access in Andhra Pradesh (see Table 1).

Table 1: Phasing open access in Andhra Pradesh

Phase	Eligibility Criteria	Commencement Date
1.	Consumers availing of power from NCE (Non Conventional Energy) developers irrespective of the quantum of contracted capacity	September 2005
2.	Contracted capacity being greater than 5 MW	September 2005
3.	Contracted capacity being greater than 2 MW	September 2006
4.	Contracted capacity being greater than 1 MW	April 2008

The Commission also finalised methods to be adopted for computation of OA Surcharge as well as framed associated regulations on 'Transmission and Wheeling charges' and 'Balancing and Settlement Code for Open Access Transactions'. The code provides for a day-ahead wheeling schedule of energy on the basis of 15-minute time blocks and monthly settlement of deviations. In addition to the above, the Commission approved the formats for long-term and short-term OA agreements as required under section 12 of the OA regulation. However, due to the existing structural limitations (transmission and distribution network congestion), OA activity from the private sector has remained absent. Apart from this structural constraint, there are several charges that an OA consumer typically pays like the cross subsidy surcharge, transmission and wheeling charges; captive charges and parallel grid operations charges etc. These charges make OA activity commercially unviable. Therefore, despite the regulation in place, there is limited interest in OA at the state level. So far (March 2009), only nine applications (130.45 MW) have been received for grant for open access in distribution, of which only two have been approved and implemented (44 MW), four are pending (82.2 MW) and three have been rejected (4.25 MW).

In the generation segment, there is limited private sector participation with the private sector contributing only approx. 18 % to total installed capacity. Of this, private sector participation is most prominent in the gas based thermal power plants and renewable energy.

3.3.3 Renewable energy

The Non-Conventional Energy Development Corporation of Andhra Pradesh Ltd. (NED-CAP) was established in 1986 by the state government as the state nodal agency for implementation of various renewable energy programs in the state. The programs are being mainly implemented in the state of Andhra Pradesh with the assistance of Ministry of Non Conventional Energy Sources (MNES) and Energy Department, Government of Andhra Pradesh. In order to promote the renewable energy program, Government of Andhra Pradesh is providing subsidy schemes in all renewable energy technologies. A total potential of 2,397 MW has been estimated for renewable energy and co-generation in the state of Andhra Pradesh. The details are given in Table 2.

Table 2: Estimated potential for renewable energy in Andhra Pradesh

Source	Potential
Wind	745 MW
Biomass	627 MW
Small Hydro	500 MW
Bagasse-based Cogeneration	350 MW
Industrial Waste	135 MW
Municipal Solid Waste	40 MW

Source: NEDCAP Survey (without year)

The Electricity Act 2003 recognises the role of renewable energy technologies for supplying power to the utility grid as well as in stand-alone systems. The Act provides for the Independent Power Producers (IPP) to set up renewable power plants for captive use, third party sale, power trading and distribution. The most important feature and the highlight of the Act is that it empowers the State Electricity Regulatory Commissions (SERCs) to promote renewable energy and specify, for purchase of electricity from renewable energy sources, a percentage of the total consumption of electricity in the area of a distribution licensee.

APERC issued the order on "Renewable Power Purchase Obligation" (RPPO) in September 2005 under section 86 (1) (e) of Electricity Act, 2003, to specify for purchase of electricity from renewable sources of energy including co-generation a percentage of the total consumption of electricity in the area of a distribution licensee. While this order was initially issued for the period 2005–06 to 2007–08, it has now been extended by the APERC till the time a revised order is issued. As per the 2005 RPPO order, it was specified that every distribution licensee shall purchase not less than five per cent (5 %) of his consumption of energy from non-conventional sources every year. Non-conventional sources include co-generation from renewable sources of energy like bagasse, mini-hydel, wind, municipal waste, industrial waste, and biomass. The total energy purchased from these sources in the states as a percentage of entire power purchase was about 4.24 % in 2007–08.

All major States have also announced feed-in-tariffs for renewable power and the recent growth of renewable power is attributed to stable regulatory policy framework. The APERC also issued the first order for determination of purchase of electrical energy generated by non-conventional energy projects in March 2004. Subsequently, in March 2009, it issued the order for determination of tariff/power purchase price for the period from 1st April 2009 to 31st March 2014 for new and renewable sources of energy, namely, bagasse based co-generation, biomass based power, industrial waste to energy, mini hydel, municipal waste to energy, and wind energy.

3.4 Supply per source, sectoral demand structure, peak deficit

Installed capacity in Andhra Pradesh summed up to 12,381.59 MW as of March 2008 and has increased by 3.2 % since 2007 (APTRANSCO, 2009). Thermal, hydel, and wind power plants were the main sources of the installed capacity in 2008. Thermal power plants comprise predominantly coal fired plants with an overall share of 6,077.95 MW, resp. 49.1 % (2007: 48.7 %).[2] Gas power plants have a share in the installed capacity of 1,638.62 MW, resp. 13.2 % (2007: 13.7 %). Andhra Pradesh is India´s biggest hydro power producer with a share of 11 % and installed capacity of 3,768.76 MW, resp. 30.4 % of power generation in Andhra Pradesh (2007: 30.7 %). The rest of 896.26 MW distributes to nuclear power plants (2.2 %), wind power (0.8 %), co-generation (3.2 %), and others, such as waste combustion (1.1 %).

Power generation is divided into the state and the private sector. Around 60 % of the installed capacity is generated by the APGENCO and around 29 % by the National Thermal Power Corporation (NTPC). Private companies provide approximately 11 % of the installed capacity.

The sectoral demand structure includes the categories domestic use, non-domestic use, industrial use, railway traction, and lighting. The entire electricity consumption in Hyderabad amounts to 2.82 TWh in 2007–08, including low tension (LT) and high tension (HT).[3] Total LT amounts to 2.19 TWh, resp. 72.3 %, whereas HT has a total

---

[2] On April 6, 2009 a sub-critical coal fired boiler of 500 MW capacity was installed and synchronised to the grid (Infraline, April 2009).

[3] Low tension operates at a maximum of 1 kilovolt (kv) for alternative current (AC) or 1.5 kv for direct current (DC). High tension means power distribution with more than 1 kv for AC resp. 1.5 kv for DC. In electric power transmission engineering, high tension is usually considered any voltage over approximately 35 kv (Gringsby et al., 2001).

share of 27.7 %. Consumption of LT is divided into different sectors. In 2007–08 the power consumption in the LT categories increased by 29 % to 2.83 TWh.[4] The biggest consumer in 2006 was the domestic sector with an overall share of 44.4 % followed by the non-domestic sector (19.0 %) and industrial use (5.6 %). Public lighting, general purpose, and temporary sum up to a share of 3.3 %. HT comprises mainly industrial consumption with a share of 26.2 % of entire consumption. Colony lighting, railway traction and temporary sum up to a share of 1.5 %.[5] Consumption of the agricultural sector was 510 GWh in 2006. The GoAP subsidises agricultural electricity consumption. Since 2004 around 95 % of agricultural customers receive electricity for free. Total electricity consumption in Andhra Pradesh since 2004 has increased with growth rates between 9.4 and 10.3 % p. a.

In Hyderabad there are at all 1,250,052 services connected (as on March 31, 2007) that correspond to an increase of 5.5 % compared to 2006. The spreading in the different categories of services is as follow: 81 % in the domestic followed with 16.8 % in the non-domestic category; about 1 % in the LT III + IV Industrial and 0.08 % in the agricultural category; almost 1 % together in the LT VI + VII + VIII categories. All services in the HT categories sum up to 0.08 % of all the services connected.[6]

Peak demand in Andhra Pradesh during the morning and the evening both have strongly increased by 37 % (morning peak) and 39 % (evening peak) whereas the peak energy deficit in Andhra Pradesh was 14 % and the total energy deficit amounted to 7.8 % in 2000.[7] The power market in Andhra Pradesh is characterised by a growing excess demand for two main reasons. Firstly, a steady growth of power demand and secondly, permanent increase of peak load since 2004 with rates between 7.8 and 9.2 % p. a. The long-term forecast by GoAP predicts additional electrical energy requirements of 8.21 % p. a. for the period 2012 to 2017.[8] Despite recently installed thermal capacity, excess demand is still growing in Andhra Pradesh and particularly in Hyderabad.

While Andhra Pradesh continues to face deficits in both energy and peak supply, there has been an improvement over the years. The deficit in energy availability, which was 8.7 % in FY 1998–99, had been reduced to 4.1 % in 2007-08. This was accomplished

---

[4] In Table A.3 in the Annex the 2008 share is listed.
[5] New consumption data for Hyderabad indicate an overall consumption 17.45 GWh per day, extrapolated from grid system particulars of March 23, 2009. Detailed data on sectoral consumption are not available for this period.
[6] Services connected in Hyderabad are listed in Table A.4 in the Annex. Eight different price categories for LT and five for HT are described in Chapter 3.5.
[7] Shukla, 2000: 7
[8] GoAP, 2007

by initiating demand side management (DSM) measures, restricting rural supply to 7 hours per day, and limiting the power purchase by DISCOMs to the approved level. Peak deficit fluctuated from 9.3 % in FY 1998–99 to 19.9 % in FY 2001–02 and 8.8 % in 2007–08. Table 3-4 give the demand and supply position in the state from FY 1998–99 to FY 2007–2008.

Table 3: Actual power supply position

Year	Requirement MU	Availability MU	Deficit MU	%
1998–99	41,958	38,293	3,665	8.7
1999–00	45,835	42,832	3,003	6.6
2000–01	47,792	44,055	3,737	7.8
2001–02	48,394	44,302	4,092	8.5
2002–03	47,223	44,014	3,209	6.8
2003–04	48,080	46,680	1,400	2.9
2004–05	50,416	50,061	355	0.7
2005–06	52,721	52,154	567	1.1
2006–07	60,964	58,280	2,684	4.4
2007–08	64,139	61,511	2,628	4.1

Source: Central Electricity Authority, Ministry of Power, GoI

Table 4: Peak demand vs. availability

Year	Requirement MW	Availability MW	Deficit MW	%
1998–99	6,770	6,139	631	9.3
1999–00	7,209	6,366	843	11.7
2000–01	8,000	6,835	1,165	14.6
2001–02	8,585	6,873	1,712	19.9
2002–03	8,491	6,858	1,633	19.2
2003–04	8,679	7,769	910	10.5
2004–05	8,093	7,903	190	2.3
2005–06	8,716	8,542	174	2.0
2006–07	10,208	8,641	1,567	15.4
2007–08	10,048	9,162	886	8.8

Source: Central Electricity Authority, Ministry of Power, GoI

3.5 Price developments

Prices are determined by APERC based on the Annual Revenue Requirement (ARR) submitted by the generation companies. In India electricity is offered at LT and HT. Low tension is available for the following eight different sub-categories: "domestic" (LT I), "non-domestic" (LT II), "industrial" (LT III), "cottage industries and dhobi ghats" (LT IV), "agriculture" (LT V), "local bodies/public lightning" (LT VI), "general purpose" (LT VII), and "temporary supply" (LT VIII). The domestic category represents all households and private electricity users whereas the non-domestic stands for all commercial energy users. The industrial low tension users are divided into two categories, and there is an additional agriculture category. The supply of energy in areas such as places of worship and government educational institutions fall into the category "general purpose" while the category "local bodies/public lightning" includes the use of energy for street lighting or public water supply (PWS) schemes. The high tension services are divided into the following five sub-categories: "industrial" (HT I), "non-industrial" (HT II), "lift irrigation scheme" (HT IV), "railway traction" (HT V), and "townships/colonies" (HT VI). Some tariffs imply an extra payment called Fuel Surcharge Adjustment (FSA). This involves variation in the fuel price for companies. The Commission approves a formula with which the companies compute the extra cost that is added to the regular tariff. The tariffs of the three other companies (APNPDCL, APSPDCL, APEPDCL) equal or come close to the tariffs specified above. Table 5 reviews all tariff categories for Andhra Pradesh.[9]

Table 5: Electricity tariff charges for Andhra Pradesh

Category	Costumer	Consumption of kWh per month	Rate per kWh	Type of charge
LT I*	Tariff for the domestic clients depends on the amount of demand.	0 – 50 units/month 51 – 100 units/month 101 – 200 units/month 201 – 300 units/month 301 units/month and more	1.45 Rs. 2.80 Rs. 3.05 Rs. 4.75 Rs. 5.50 Rs.	MMC[a]: Single phase <250 W = 25 Rs. >250 W = 50 Rs. Three phase: 150 Rs.
LT II*	Tariff for the non-domestic (commercial) clients.	0 – 50 units/month 51 units/month and more	3.85 Rs. 6.20 Rs.	MMC: Single phase: 65 Rs. Three phase: 200 Rs.
LT III (A)*	Applicable to the supply of energy for the Industrial normal category (up to 75 Horse Power (HP)).	Normal Optional Off season for seasonal loads Sugarcane crushing Pisciculture, prawn culture (>10HP)	3.75 Rs. 3.75 Rs. 4.40 Rs. 0.50 Rs. 0.90 Rs.	Extra charge: 37 Rs./HP/month 100 Rs./kVA/month – –
LT III (B)	Applicable to the supply of energy for the Industrial optional category (75 HP to 150 HP).	Normal Off season for seasonal loads	3.75 Rs. 4.40 Rs.	Demand charge: 100 Rs./kVA/month of contracted demand

[9] At an exchange rate of 1.486 euros for 100 Rs. as of May 2009.

Category	Costumer	Consumption of kWh per month	Rate per kWh	Type of charge
LT IV*	Tariff for the cottage industry and dobhi gaits.	For all units consumed	1.80 Rs.	Fixed charge: 10 Rs./HP/month of contracted load (min. 30 Rs./month)
LT V (A)*	Tariff for agriculture with DSM measures	Dry land farmers (connection up to 3) and wet land farmers (Holdings up to 2.5 Acres)	free of charge	Fixed charge: –
		Dry land farmers (connection >3)	0.20 Rs.	210 Rs./HP/year
		Wet land farmers (Holdings >2.5 Acres)	0.20 Rs.	210 Rs./HP/year
		Corporate farmers & IT assesses	1.00 Rs	–
	Tariff for agriculture without DSM measures.	Dry land farmers (connection up to 3)	0.20 Rs.	210 Rs./HP/year
		Wet land farmers (holdings up to 2.5 acres)	0.20 Rs.	210 Rs./HP/year
		Dry land farmers (connection >3)	0.50 Rs.	525 Rs./HP/year
		Wet land farmers (holdings >2.5 Acres)	0.50 Rs.	525 Rs./HP/year
		Corporate farmers & IT assesses	2.00 Rs.	–
LT V (B)	Agriculture tariff, out of turn allotment - Tatkal scheme with DSM measures.	Normal	0.20 Rs.	–
LT VI	Tariff for street light services depending on local bodies.	Minor panchayats	1.56 Rs.	MMC: 2 Rs./Point
		Major panchayats	2.08 Rs.	2 Rs./Point
		Nagarpalikas & municipalities (Gr.3)	2.74 Rs.	6 Rs./Point
		Municipalities (Gr.1&2)	3.26 Rs.	6 Rs./Point
		Municipalities selection	3.53 Rs.	6 Rs./Point
		Corporations	3.79 Rs.	6 Rs./Point
	Tariff for the PWS schemes depending on local bodies.	Minor / major panchayats (up to 2,500 units p.a.)	0.20 Rs.	Fixed charge: –
		Minor / major panchayats (>2,500 units p.a.)	0.50 Rs.	20 Rs./HP/month
		All types of municipalities (up to 1,000 units/month)	3.75 Rs.	20 Rs./HP/month
		All types of municipalities (balance units/month)	4.05 Rs.	20 Rs./HP/month
		Corporations (up to 1000 units/month)	4.05 Rs.	20 Rs./HP/month
		Corporation (balance units/month)	4.60 Rs.	
LT VII*	Applicable to the supply of energy for general purpose such as places of worship and government educational institutions.	All units	4 Rs.	MMC: Single phase: 50 Rs. Three phase: 150 Rs.
LT VIII*	LT temporary supply for all categories other than agriculture	All units	6.20 Rs.	MMC: 125 Rs./KW/month
	LT temporary supply for agriculture purposes.	All units	2.30 Rs.	100 Rs./HP/month
HT I	Tariff for the industry sector (general) (possible discount on energy rates about 25 %)*		(per unit)	Demand charge:
		132 kV and above	2.80 Rs.	250 Rs./kVA/month
		33 kV	3.10 Rs.	230 Rs./kVA/month
		11 kV and below	3.30 Rs.	195 Rs./kVA/month
		All units	2.55 Rs.	–
	Tariff for the ferro alloy units industry (possible discount on energy rates about 25 %)	132 kV and above	3.65 Rs.	250 Rs./kVA/month
		33 kV	3.90 Rs.	230 Rs./kVA/month

Category	Costumer	Consumption of kWh per month	Rate per kWh	Type of charge
		11 kV and below	4.40 Rs.	195 Rs./kVA/month
	Tariff for seasonal industries.*			
HT II*	Tariff applicable to non-industries.	132 kV and above	(per unit) 3.65 Rs.	Demand charge: 250 Rs./kVA/month
		33 kV	3.90 Rs.	230 Rs./kVA/month
		11 kV and below	4.40 Rs.	195 Rs./kVA/month
HT IV (A)*	Tariff applicable to governmental lift irrigation schemes.		2.36 Rs.	–
HT IV (B)	Tariff to agriculture.		0 Rs.	–
HT V	Tariff applicable to railway traction loads.	All units	4.20 Rs.	–
HT VI*	Tariff applicable exclusively for townships and residential colonies.	All units	3.50 Rs.	–

[a] monthly minimum charge; * Fuel Surcharge Adjustment extra as applicable.

Source: data from APERC (2008), APCPDCL (2009)

The average cost of power production differs among the types of power plants. With 0.24 Rs./unit average cost, the hydel power plants from APGENCO are the most effective ones in the power producing mix followed with distance by the gas power plant of APGPCL with 1.41 Rs./Unit. The thermal power stations both at APGENCO and others have average costs between 1.72 to 1.98 Rs./Unit. In contrast, the independent power producers attain average costs of 2.35 Rs./Unit while the non-conventional energy plants (e.g. biomass, municipal waste to energy, wind power, mini hydel) and the mini power plants attain average costs of 3.06 Rs./Unit. All APGENCO power plants achieve average costs of 1.52 Rs./Unit.

In 2008-09, the total subsidies for APCPDCL in FY amount to 4.87 million €. About 70 % ($\approx$ 3.4 million €) of them are granted to the irrigation and agriculture sector (LT V and HT IV) and about 27 % (1.3 million €) to the domestic sector (LT I). This value is small in comparison to subsidies given to the other distribution companies in AP. In receiving 111.3 million euros, the northern distribution company APNPDCL collects about 23 times more; 63 % go to the irrigation and agriculture sector and 23 % to the domestic sector. In the south, APSPDCL pays about 12 times more (59.5 million €) subsidies than APCPDCL, 60 % for the irrigation and agriculture sector and 25 % for the domestic sector.

4 The structure of electricity generation, transmission, distribution, consumption

As aforementioned, the energy sector of Andhra Pradesh is unbundled into independent state owned and–in case of generation–private companies. APGENCO is responsible for power generation and covers around 60 % of the power generation in the state. APTRANSCO is a transmission company; it distributes the power generated by the NTPC and by IPPs. It covers the remaining 40 % share of power generation together with private, co-operative power, and captive generators. The four distribution companies (DISCOM) deliver power to the end customers. APCPDCL is responsible for the Hyderabad region. The power sector in Andhra Pradesh has one of the highest plant load factors in India but the transmission and distribution sectors still face high losses and a poor billing performance (Lamb, 2006: 40). Tariffs remain highly cross-subsidised. Due to full subsidies for agricultural power use, prices for industry are comparatively high in Andhra Pradesh. The regulator APERC sets end market prices and has the authority to regulate market access through licensing (Sarkar, Deb, Sundararaman, 2002: 23–24, Sarkar et al., 2002: 45).

The planning for the expansion of generation, transmission, and distribution capacities in the power sector is primarily based on load forecasts provided by the distribution companies. The APTRANSCO compiles the load forecasts from all four DISCOMs and plans the required transmission and generation capacity in the state accordingly. APTRANSCO submits the plan to the APERC for the control period, as approval of investment plans falls in APERC's responsibility. At present, APTRANSCO has submitted a plan for the control period 2009–14 to the APERC.

The chapter is divided into three sub-chapters in order to reflect the structure of the energy sector in Andhra Pradesh. In the following sub-chapters, we describe the composition of the energy sector on the country and municipal level. Each sub-chapter gives a detailed description of the sector, including an evaluation of data quantity and quality as well as cross-references to the database in the annex.

4.1 Power generation in Andhra Pradesh

4.1.1 Description and salient features of APGENCO and private generation companies

After the Government of Andhra Pradesh unbundled the energy sector, the state-owned utility APGENCO, responsible for the operation of state controlled thermal and hydro power plants, was formed out of the former APSEB in the fiscal year 2000–01. APGENCO has an installed capacity of 7,527.5 MW in Andhra Pradesh; the overall power supply was 33.29 TWh in 2008, which accounts for a share of 50.4 % of power generation in Andhra Pradesh.[10] Moreover, it is one of the largest power generation companies in India. Evolving new capacities for thermal and hydro power plants during the last years have led to the highest amount of power generation since APGENCO's inception. The largest share of power generation in Andhra Pradesh comes from thermal power plants, which account for 70.5 %, where 35.4 % comes from the APGENCO power plants. About 23.7 % of power generation comes from hydro power where APGENCO stands for nearly all the share. Recently APGENCO has turned into a profit making firm and has earned a net profit of approx. 29.4 million € in the fiscal year 2007–08, wiping out the net losses incurred during the fiscal years 2004–05 to 2006-07.[11] APGENCO capacity performance data show hydro power remaining at constant capacity levels while thermal capacity is steadily growing and wind power is still insignificant.[12]

4.1.2 Generation by source in Andhra Pradesh and description of generation plants

The power generation mix consists of 51.3 % thermal and 48.6 % hydel power plants. Furthermore, APGENCO operates a 2 MW wind farm. Five thermal plants with an installed capacity of 3,862.5 MW are owned, operated, and maintained by APGENCO. The largest thermal power plant called Vijayawada Thermal Power Station has a total installed capacity of 1,760 MW and the smallest, called Ramagundam "B" Thermal Power Station, of 62.5 MW whereas the other three plants have a capacity ranging between 500 MW to 840 MW. All thermal power stations are coal operated. In addition, APGENCO owns, operates, and maintains 18 hydel plants, including three mini hydel power stations that are constructed to use water releases through irrigation canals. There

---

[10] See Table A.1 in the Annex.
[11] www.apgenco.gov.in, 2009.
[12] Future investments by APGENCO are listed in Table 4-1.

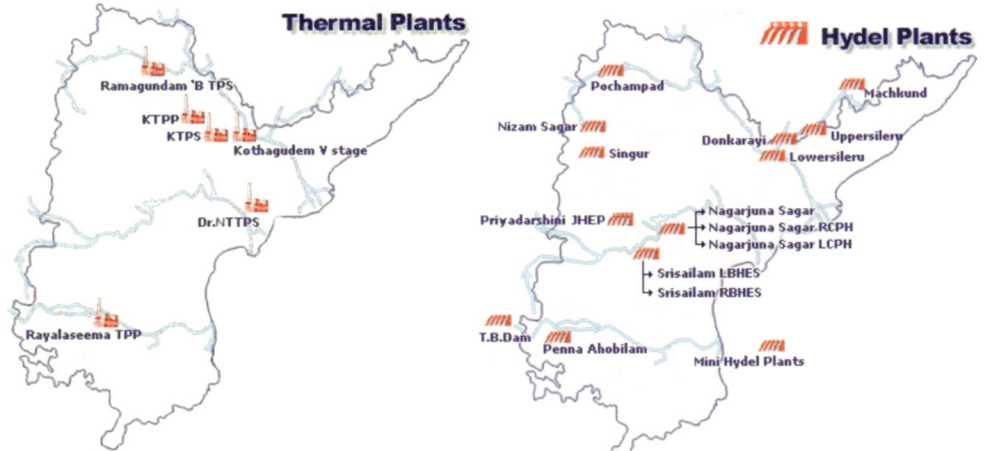

Figure 1: APGENCO power plants in Andhra Pradesh
Source: http://apgenco.gov.in/inner.asp?frm=our_pow_plants_thermal1

are five hydel plants that have an installed capacity well above 100 MW. The largest one, Srisailam Left Bank Powerhouse, has an installed capacity of 900 MW, and the smallest plant, Chettipeta Mini Hydro Station, operates with two units with 500 KW of installed capacity each.[13]

Another public power corporation operating in AP is NTPC, which is the largest power generation company in India.[14] With its two large coal power plants NTPC stands for 23.3 % of the total installed capacity in AP. The Ramagundam Thermal Power Plant with an installed capacity of 2,600 MW represents the largest power plant in AP. The second largest power plant is the Simhadri TPP and has an installed capacity of 1,000 MW. Two units of 39 MW each at the Priyadarshini Jurala Hydro Electric Project, which is projected to have a total capacity of 234 MW, started operations 2008. The other units are still under construction and are scheduled to go online in 2009.

4.1.3 Investments

In recent years APGENCO has launched several new thermal and hydro projects as illustrated in Table 7. Five thermal projects (one gas and four coal fired plants) are in progress and scheduled for commission between 2009 and 2011 with an overall capacity of 5,200 MW. Five hydro projects are in progress and scheduled for commission by 2009

---

[13] All APGENCO power plants are listed in the Annex.
[14] 89,5 % of the equity is held by the Indian Government (ntpc.co.in).

and 2010 respectively with an additional capacity of approx. 533 MW. The APGENCO projects have an overall capacity of 6,943 MW and involve an estimated expenditure of 3.3 billion €. An amount of 0.475 billion euros (14.4 %) is financed by the Indian government through Power Finance Corporation (PFC) and 0.32 billion € (9.7 %) are financed by Rural Electrification Corporation (REC), which is a wholly owned company of the Government of India.

Table 7: New APGENCO investment projects

Project	Time schedule	Investment (mil. €)	MW
Krishnapatnam Thermal Power Station	2010/2011	1,253.0	1,600
Priyadarshini Jurala Hydro Electric Project (Unit 3-6)	2009/2010	81.3	156
Nagarjunasagar Tail Pond Dam Power House	2009	69.1	50
Lower Jurala H.E.P.	2009	131.5	240
Kakatiya Thermal Power Plant Stage I	2010	319.5	1,600
Kakatiya Thermal Power Plant Stage II	2010	304.6	500
Gas Based Power Station at Karimnagar	2009	820.3	2,100
KTPS Stage VI	2009	321.6	500
Pochampad HES Unit IV	2009	3.0	9
Total		3,303.9	6,755

Source: www.apind.gov.in/whyap1.html

1.25 billion € (37.9 %) are co-financed by PFC and KfW, and a joint venture of PFC and REC plans to invest 1.26 billion € (38 %). In addition, there are private investments in mini-hydro power (40 million €), wind power plants (51.1 million €), bio mass (53.2 million €), bio-co-generation (29.4 million €), industrial and municipal solid waste (1.6 million €). Public investments in wind power plants add up to 2.5 million €.

Moreover, Coastal Andhra Power Limited (CAPL) is a wholly owned subsidiary of Reliance Power Ltd. since January 2008. CAPL's is responsible for building, owning, operating, and maintaining the Krishnapatnam Ultra Mega Power Project at Nellore District in Andhra Pradesh. The 4,000 MW project is scheduled to be fully commissioned (last stage) in October 2015. Reliance Power Ltd. has won the bidding process with 0.03 €/kWh.[15] A power purchase agreement (PPA) has been signed between the states Andhra Pradesh, Tamil Nadu, Karnataka, and Maharashtra. Andhra Pradesh, the lead procurer, will receive 40 % of the power generated at the facility and the other states 20 % each.[16]

---

[15] This amount corresponds to an overall investment of approx. 1.2 billion €.
[16] www.reliancepower.co.in/html/sub_capl.html

In addition to APGENCO, six private companies (IPPs) currently operate power plants in Andhra Pradesh, with an overall capacity of 2,981.6 MW including mini-hydel.[17] They are GVK Industries Ltd., LANCO Power, Spectrum Power Generation Ltd., Reliance Energy Ltd., GMR group, and Konaseema Gas Power Ltd.

GVK Industries Ltd. specializes in infrastructure and urban infrastructure development projects in India, particularly in the area of power, airports, roads, hospitality, services, and manufacturing.[18] GVK set up India's first independent power project, the 2,167 MW Jegurupadu Combined Cycle Power Plant in Andhra Pradesh. In January 2006, a 220 MW expansion facility followed at the same site (commenced operations in April 2009) and the 464 MW Gautami Power Ltd. Facility was installed, a combined cycle power plant located in Peddapuram near Kakinada in Andhra Pradesh.[19] GVKs´ overall power generation capacity in Andhra Pradesh amounts to 9,010 MW.

LANCO Power is part of the conglomerate Lanco Infratech Ltd. with a spread of projects across India.[20] LANCO Kondapalli Power Pvt. Ltd. (LKPPL) runs the Kondapalli power plant stage I to III. The 368 MW unit is a combined cycle power plant operating on natural gas as primary fuel. LKPPL invested 163.5 million € based on a power purchase agreement (PPA) for a period of 15 years. LKPPL supplies power to APTRANSCO. Stage II of Kondapalli is commissioned and extends the installed capacity to 736 MW.

Spectrum Power Generation Ltd. (SPGL) owns and operates a gas-fired combined cycle 208 MW power plant and supplies to APTRANSCO. SPGL was incorporated in 1992 and is based in Hyderabad.

Reliance Energy Ltd. is an Indian group running several power plants through subsidiaries across India. BSES Andhra Energy Limited is an associated company of Reliance Power Ltd. Since 2003 the company runs Smalkot East Godavari, a 220 MW dual fuel based combined power station and transmits power to APTRANSCO.

The GMR group is an Indian infrastructure company with interests in energy too. The power generation project in Andhra Pradesh, located at Vermagiri, close to Rajahmundry, is a natural gas based thermal power plant with an installed capacity of 388.5 MW. In addition to the existing power plant, they are considering to build the first floating power plant (200 MW) next to the port city Kakinada in Andhra Pradesh.

Finally, the gas based 460 MW Konaseema Power Plant started power generation in March 2009. Completed 2006, the plant has lain idle since then due to a lack of fuel.

---

[17] For detailed information compare Table A.2 in the Annex.
[18] www.gvk.com
[19] www.inrnews.com/realestateproperty/india/sez/gvk_signs_mou_with_tamil_nadu.html
[20] www.lancogroup.com

Konaseema Gas Power Ltd. is its operator and plans to expand the facility to 820 MW. In addition to this, private companies operate several mni-hydel power projects with an overall capacity of 69.1 MW (APGENCO, 2007, file 4.8).

In 2008 the power supply deficit in Andhra Pradesh has increased to approx. 2,500 MW.[21] Additional power supply requires investments in new thermal, nuclear, and hydro power stations. Current investments indicate investment requirements of 0.6 million €/MW on average. This restricts the scope for additional investments in power generation capacity.

4.1.4 Pollution standards

High efficiency electro-static precipitators (ESPs) have been installed to control suspended particulate matter (SPM) in flue gas. All new plants are designed for a SPM level of 100 mg/Nm3 (norm volume). Old units have been or are being upgraded for 50/115 mg/Nm3 against the APPCB limit of 115 mg/Nm3. Controllers have been installed for improvement of collection efficiency and reduction of power consumption. Online flue gas dust monitoring systems have been installed at several thermal power stations. Coal plant and other plant effluent is treated in the settling tanks. Plant and colony sewage is treated in the septic tanks. Effective de-cantation systems are provided in the ash ponds to control suspended solids. Suspended solids in the ash pond outlet effluent are below 50 ppm against a standard of 100 ppm.

4.2 Power transmission and distribution in Andhra Pradesh and Hyderabad

4.2.1 Power transmission in Andhra Pradesh

After the reform of the energy sector in Andhra Pradesh in 1998, the transmission sector was unbundled and is now operated by the APTRANSCO, which has its headquarters in Hyderabad and generates an annual required revenue of 4 million €, 68 % of which is for personnel costs.[22] The company operates nine substations with 400 kV, 92 substations with 220 kV, and 267 11 kV substations with overall lines of 30,293.5 Ckm.[23] The grid

---

[21] Power supply deficit in Hyderabad in relation to Andhra Pradesh might differ. Actual data on power supply deficits and grid capacity investments are not yet available for APCPDCL and in particular for Hyderabad.

[22] APTRANSCO, 2007, Analysis of Performance

[23] Ckm means circuit kilometres and are defined as route kilometres of revenue producing circuits in service, determined by measuring the length in kilometres of the actual path the transmission medium follows, i.e. the product of the number of lines and the length in km.

consumption in March 2009 amounts to 191 GWh per day including power generation from APGENCO, NTPC, and the IPPs. Based on data for January 2009, overall demand for electricity in Andhra Pradesh amounts to 6.19 TWh whereas available supply adds up to only 5.86 TWh. This indicates a 0.33 TWh deficit, respectively 5.33 % of entire electricity demand. At 99.97 %, grid availability in Andhra Pradesh is comparatively high due to expansion projects and best maintenance practices (Koteswara, Krishna, 2007: 78).

There are two different sorts of losses in the energy sector: first, transmission and distribution (T & D) losses and, second, commercial losses. T & D are physical losses, corresponding to "joule effects" or heat losses, arising from the flow of current in the electrical system. APTRANSCO has successfully made investments to continuously reduce transmission losses in Andhra Pradesh in recent years. After the unbundling of the energy sector, transmission losses were brought down from nearly 9 % in 2000 to approx. 4 % in 2007, involving investments of about 420 million € in total.[24] To meet the growing power demand and to close the increasing gap between electricity demand and supply, APTRANSCO has planned to invest around 750 million € in 94 EHT substations and 6,266 Ckm of EHT lines.

The Asian Development Bank supported by Powergrid has started to invest in grid strengthening in Tamil Nadu, Andhra Pradesh, and Union Territory of Pondicherry with 98-cct-km of 400 kV transmission lines and 1,260 MVA of 400/200 kV substation capacity added. The project volume is 20.3 million €. It is part of a 405.8 million € package of grid investments in India mainly financed by the Asia Development Bank, with an overall share of 285.8 million € and by Powergrid contributing 120 million €.[25]

The power demand surplus is an increasing problem for APTRANSCO and the distribution companies, such as APCPDCL responsible for Hyderabad. First, demand has continuously increased and has reached its peak in March 2008 with 195 GWh per day. In 2008, APTRANSCO simultaneously purchased power amounting to 17 GWh from six states GWh to reduce the 5 % supply gap and paid a sum of 2.23 million € per day towards this bulk purchase. Temporarily, the shortage peaked at 29 GWh per day. To counter this development, APTRANSCO would have to invest in additional capacity to the tune of 1,000 MW to generate 17 GWh per day.

A second problem is the breakdown of power plants feeding into the grid of APTRANSCO. For example, during the year 2008 several breakdowns of thermal and nuc-

---

[24] Koteswara, Krishna, 2007: 78.
[25] At an exchange rate of 1.399 USD for 1 € (http://de.finance.yahoo.com/waehrungen/)

lear power plants from generation companies in other countries and from central power stations amounted to an overall loss of more than 1,200 MW. The power utility was able to meet the high demand in spite of the state grid losing an installed capacity of 200 MW following the tripping of the three units at the Kothagudem Thermal Power Station. To reduce shortage APTRANSCO recently has launched efficiency programs to reduce demand instead of power supply. With the Energy Efficiency Cooperation (EECO) Cell, launched at the end of the year 2008, APTRANSCO in consultation with stakeholders, first, is going to increase capacity building and dissemination measures, along with creating awareness across all categories of electricity consumers and aiding and advising power utilities in achieving energy efficiency and conservation of energy. Second, the program aims at improvements in energy management and in monitoring energy consumption. Moreover, the EECO Cell is charged with the task of promoting awareness of CDM and R&D activities for energy efficiency and conservation. The budget for EECO in the fiscal year of 2008–09 is initially financed by APTRANSCO, which has to be reimbursed by the four DISCOMs as they are the main beneficiaries of the intended measure.

4.2.2 Power distribution in Andhra Pradesh and Hyderabad

As part of the reform of the Andhra Pradesh electricity sector in 1998, APCPDCL has been commissioned with the operation and administration of electricity distribution in the central region of Andhra Pradesh encompassing the districts of Hyderabad, Medak Sangareddi, Rangareddi, Nalgonda, Mahbubnagar, Kurnool, and Anantapur to serve the power requirements of 57.4 million consumers (APCPDCL, 2007). The company is charged with the task of distributing electricity to customers at an affordable price. The infrastructure facilities in the operating area amount to 972 nos. of 33/11 kV substations, 1,459 nos. of power transformers, 522 nos. of 33 kV feeders, 3,676 nos. of 11 kV feeders and around 160,983 nos. of distribution transformers of various capacities. APCPDCL purchases electricity directly from APTRANSCO, which buys electricity from APGENCO, central generators, and IPP´s. Up to now APCPDCL has electrified about 6,500 villages, 25,600 hamlets, and different sorts of colonies.

The following initiatives have been taken by APCPDCL in its area of operation:

- Continuous monitoring of interruptions and voltage on industrial feeders and designating special officers for these feeders
- Continuous monthly energy audit of feeders

- Deployments of electronic meters for high value customers
- Consumer Analysis Tool (CAT) has been set up to track billing irregularities and metering errors
- Transformer Management Information System (TMIS) to track the maintenance schedule of the distribution transformer and meters
- A citizen's charter has been introduced and its implementation is monitored through call centres
- On-line billing collection facility has been made available in Hyderabad city and all the towns through e-seva centres
- Meetings with consumers held every month at circle and division level, major issues raised are billing complaints and delay in replacement of Distribution Transformer (DTRs) in rural areas

Some of the initiatives in APCPDCL to improve Quality of Service are the following:

Integrated Customer Service Centres (ICSCs): are equipped with trained operators and IT infrastructure to address consumer complaints and service issues such as meter correction, O & M complaints, address correction, shifting meter, etc. New Services are being released only through ICSCs and senior management monitors this process on a monthly basis.

Fuse of Call Centres [FOCs]: every sub-division office, has a call centre to address operations and maintenance complaints.

155333: A 6-digit telephone 155333 with 30 numbers of dedicated telephones are provided for the customer fuse-off-call grievances round the clock. The electricity consumer complaints cell at SCADA (Supervisory Control and Date Acquisition) operates with 75 operators to attend to such calls throughout the day and night.

SCADA centre provides the real time information as well as historical data, which is utilised for fault analysis, and also for closely monitoring the supply for essential services and important public programs. Load shedding also can be programmed in a systematic manner duly avoiding inconvenience to the consumer during shortage of power supply and exigencies. Controlling and monitoring of distribution system (mostly 33 kV network) at 33 & 11 kV levels is done remotely from SCADA centre, which has improved the reliability and quality of supply, by reducing the break down time and prompt restoration of supply in case of outages. Another focus of the background study by milestone two is to monitor and evaluate the activities of the DISCOMs and to combine them with own developments of demonstration projects.

4.3 Power consumption in Hyderabad

This section of the background study describes the consumption patterns in the sectors public, industry, small and medium-sized enterprises, and private households. It is followed by analysis of behaviour of energy consumers aimed at identifying determinants of inefficient energy use and drivers for efficiency improvements such as institutional and technological changes. In the descriptive section we examine the costs of energy use in the public and private sectors and the technological options for substituting inefficient resource input. In the analytical section we apply scientific methods designed to reveal preferences of consumers across the whole range of energy services and to reveal determinants of consumption and investment behaviour. The main objective of this part of the background study is to calculate willingness to pay values for efficiency improvements and their determinants in order to identify options for pilot projects in the energy sector. The analysis of consumer behaviour pays particular attention to the needs and demands of the poor in order to examine specific requirements of technology adoption and financial concepts in co-operation with public and private stakeholders.

As mentioned above, capacity of energy generation and transmission fail to keep up with the growing demand for energy and electricity in particular. The growth rate of installed capacity between 2007 and 2008 is less than 1 % whereas the population growth rate is at nearly 4 % per year in average. Furthermore, transmission and distribution losses sum up to more than 20 %.[26] On the supply side, hydro capacity is limited and accommodating a steady growth of power demand requires new fossil power plants. However, even new 500 MW coal fired power stations will each contribute a minimum of 2 Mt CO_2 per year to climate change, i.e. each installation will have significant climate change impacts. Due to insufficient generation capacity there has been an acute shortage of power supply. This raises the question whether additional capacity of central power generation is sufficient to solve the growing problem of power shortages. On the other hand, organised efforts on part of the private sector and single households bears major potential for mitigating the supply problem and the problem of high emissions. For example, energy saving measures and decentralised power generation are growing options for households and small-scale enterprises. The analyses for the background study are

---

[26] UN, 2001; APCPDCL, 2008

the main focus of the second milestone by September 2010. They are concerned with examining feasible options for reducing power supply gaps that involve activities in the private sector. A survey of consumption patterns and preferences for measures to reduce power breakdowns will give insights into private investment behaviour of households and small-scale enterprises (service and production).[27] Based on this data, we will analyse the regulatory system governing the energy sector in Andhra Pradesh for drivers of and obstacles to technical solutions.

Exploratory interviews and choice experiments will be conducted to identify attributes and preferences concerning energy efficient technologies and services, which will then be analysed employing state-of-the-art econometric methods. An explorative study on consumer needs in Hyderabad conducted in April 2009 together with Work Package 4 will provide first insights into the analysis of the energy market in Hyderabad. Data about the growing demand for electrical energy and importance of private electricity generating capacities in Hyderabad indicate that, given the aforementioned problems, many of the households and industries have already developed highly individual coping strategies in order to deal with bad quality, unannounced power cuts, and in-transparent billing. Given the scenario of rapid growth, these individual strategies have already and will very likely lead to an uncontrolled rank growth of private power generation. The impact of non-coordinated development of generation on emissions and the efficiency of energy will be estimated in the analytical section of the background study. This will provide a basis for the further development of pilot projects in the energy sector and for identification of drivers and barriers for efficiency improvements in energy use.

Regarding the outcome expected from the megacity project in terms of sustainable and energy efficient strategies for adaptation and mitigation of climate change impacts, priority is given to determinants of consumer behaviour in different areas. This involves, first, efficiency effects of APERC's regulatory measures on investment incentives for firms and for consumption behaviour of public and private households, and second, market driven effects on firms' investment activities and on consumption behaviour of public and private households. Knowledge of individual willingness to pay for investing in energy efficient technologies along with information on individual expectations of price developments and availability of technological innovations are required to assess any public and private activity towards efficiency improvements in the energy sector. Economic market research on environmental behaviour of consumers provides appropri-

---

[27] Data survey and analysis are based on state-of-the-art methods and instruments applied in recently conducted studies, such as Bollino, 2009; Morrison, Nalder, 2009; Grösche, Vance, 2009; Rommel, Meyerhoff, 2007 and Rommel, Meyerhoff, 2009.

ate techniques like the contingent valuation method and choice experiments to reveal consumer preferences for market goods and for public goods, such as security of electricity supply and mitigation of environmental damage. Interview design in both cases will be based on the findings gained from the analysis of the energy sector as described in the Chapters 4.1 and 4.2. With the results of analysis of consumer behaviour in the energy market we are able to identify needs of energy efficiency measures and technologies with respect to income structures. Finally, the consumer behaviour analyses complete the background study and provide data for a cost-benefit analysis of institutional and economic changes, such as qualitative and quantitative changes in tariffs, and gives support to the development of demonstration projects.

5 Options for efficiency improvements in the energy sector

In addition to the growing gap of power supply the energy sector of Andhra Pradesh and particularly of Hyderabad faces several problems of inefficiency as aforementioned. These deficits can be summarised first, into general deficits resulting from policy measures beyond the energy sector and, second, into sector specific shortcomings:

General reasons for inefficient energy use:

- A significant share of the state funds is used in providing subsidy to the agricultural consumers in form of free power. Therefore, pricing mechanisms are not based on cost covering revenues and farmers have no incentives for efficient energy use. The grant of these subsidies with an amount of 3.4 million € in FY 2008–09 causes high opportunity costs because this budget is not available for funds carrying out energy efficiency measures.

- High taxation of energy efficient appliances such as VAT on compact fluorescent lamp (CFL) at 12.5 %.

Sector specific shortcomings:

- High volume of power consumption in the water sector due to inefficient irrigation, i.e. energy taking pumping solutions, and shortfalls of drinking water supply. Fully subsidised power for most farmers together with restricted power supply to rural areas prevents incentives for efficient use of electricity.

- High tariffs charged from the industrial and commercial consumers provide them with enough incentive for adoption of energy efficiency measures in their processes. However, no significant efforts are being undertaken with regard to promotion of energy efficiency in the domestic sector.
- Transmission and distribution losses are approximately 20 %, however it does not include losses from agriculture, because agriculture supply is unmetered.
- Solar streetlights cause very high investments for purchase and maintenance. Moreover, timers have not been installed on streetlights due to theft problems and insufficient political will to curtail electricity theft in the city.
- There is no subsidy from the state government for the use of solar water heaters.

Predominantly in the city of Hyderabad additional inefficiencies arise in the building sector due to insufficient promotion of green buildings providing high standards of energy savings. The checklist of the GHMC does not encompass measures to reduce energy consumption, waste and water management in a more sustainable way. The existing bye laws as well as the master plan remain silent about energy conservation in buildings. Additional barriers for the construction of green buildings are higher incremental costs, builders are also reluctant to adopt any strict regulations and a low level of awareness about advantages of green buildings. Also general lack of awareness about the concept of energy conservation and efficiency, various government policies regarding energy conservation among the users of various kinds of buildings is observed. As consequence, most of the upcoming buildings in the city are energy-inefficient (urban heat-island effect). Although Hyderabad already has some LEED rated buildings[28], there are also listed energy auditors and few verifiers for the rating systems in the city that have not become very popular.

Incentives are provided to encourage use of solar energy in the state of Andhra Pradesh. A rebate of 10 % in the property tax is given by the local authority to owner of buildings that install and use solar heating and lighting system.

Further, the Andhra Pradesh Revised Common Building Rules, 2008 applicable to all municipal corporations and the urban development authorities, in the state except

---

[28] The Leadership in Energy and Environmental Design (LEED) is a rating system for green buildings, developed by the U.S. Green Building Council (USGBC). LEED provides various standards for environ-mentally sustainable construction. Since its inception in 1998, LEED has grown to encompass more than 14,000 projects in 50 U.S. The attribute of LEED is that it is an open and transparent process where the technical criteria proposed by the LEED committees are publicly reviewed for approval by membership organisations (USGBC, 2009).

Greater Hyderabad Municipal Corporation, Greater Visakhapatnam Municipal Corporation, Vijayawada Municipal Corporation, Guntur Municipal Corporation, Hyderabad Airport Development Authority (HADA), Visakhapatnam Urban Development Authority (VUDA), and Vijayawada Guntur Tenali Mangalagiri Urban Development Authority (VGTMUDA) areas requires that the building requirements and standards other than heights and setbacks specified in the national building code, 2005 shall be complied with. Under these standards, compliance of national building code provisions for amenities and facilities in all high rise buildings requires that all such buildings shall be provided with solar water heating system in the building and solar lighting in the site for outdoor lighting, etc. and give a bank guarantee to this effect to the sanctioning authority for compliance of the same.

A lot of initiatives have been undertaken by the utility in order to improve delivery of services in terms of energy efficiency improvements such as the following:

- Renewable Energy
    - Renewable Purchase Quota set at 5 % by the commission for the financial year 2007–08.
    - RPO quota is being fixed after taking into consideration first, the potential of renewable energy in the state, second, PPAs already signed by the utilities and the projected PPAs by the utilities and third, licensee ability to absorb high tariff of renewable, profitability of both distributor and the utility has to be taken into account.
    - All the utilities together have to achieve the quota as the source of renewable are not distributed proportionally.

- Street Lighting
    - Street lighting is divided into 27 packages and private contractors are called on tender basis for its maintenance and operation. New installation is done by GHMC.

- Waste to energy
    - GHMC has an agreement for supplying waste to various companies including SELCO[29], which is involved in waste to energy projects. The waste generated in the city is supplied by GHMC to the waste processing plant of SELCO.

---

[29] SELCO International Ltd. is a Hyderabad based company with core business focus on Municipal Solid Waste (MSW) management.

After, processing the waste, it is transported to the power plant by SELCO on its own transportation costs.

- Distribution System Planning

    - Trend analysis is used for demand estimation and system planning is based on load forecast.
    - Distribution system planning is dynamic, what load will be required in future is not easy to forecast. So, a maximum of three year planning is done.
    - In case of industrial development in the state, Andhra Pradesh Industrial Infrastructure Corporation Ltd. (APIIC) informs the utility regarding the new activities planned in the city and accordingly utility plans for the development of its network.
    - Being a notified slum, electricity supply is metered and streetlights are installed in the slums.

Load shedding is very minimal throughout the state and there is a good mix of electricity generation sources. Provision of free agricultural power is the major issue facing the electricity sector in the state. For this reason, lesser funds are available for carrying out activities such as energy efficiency. Not much effort has been invested in promoting demand side management. The Commission is of the view that there being a separate energy conservation act the responsibility of carrying out these services rest with the state designated agencies. On the other hand, SDA (State Designated Agency) takes the view that it can engage in such activities only on a limited scale due to the non-availability of funds; therefore it rests on the utilities to promote such measures.

In terms of innovative practices for green buildings, the development authority is interested in adopting measures to promote sustainable buildings both for new buildings as well as existing old ones. It has already initiated a program to come up with environmental building regulations and guidelines geared toward promoting energy conservation in buildings, efficient water, waste, and sewage management for buildings and at city level, and toward preventing pollution caused by the construction and operation of buildings. Hyderabad is one of the only two cities in India to keep a register of heritage buildings and the only city to do so concerning rock formations. However, all on-going construction takes place with no consideration for such formations, and, consequently, the city is experiencing a rapid loss of such beautiful heritage spots.

6 Efficiency monitoring and further steps of the background study

Up to this point the results of the background study indicate power supply gaps and unused potential for energy savings as main reasons for inefficiencies, such as breakdowns, high emissions, and resource degradation. Inefficient structures in the energy sector refer mainly to the huge and growing electricity supply gap, actually more than 4.5 %, stemming from growing demand, with high T & D and commercial losses, and, finally, insufficient rules and incentives for efficient energy use. Hence, efficiency improvements through awareness and capacity building barely exist. At the political level these deficits have been realised and efficiency measures have been launched, such as awareness and capacity building for firms and households and investments in electrification programs. However, incentives for green buildings and other energy saving technologies are at an early stage and mainly provided without sufficient political thrust to support them. Therefore, these activities seem to be insufficient to solve shortcomings and address welfare losses resulting from high mitigation costs and economic losses due to restricted power use. Moreover, attempts of the DISCOMs to increase incentives for electricity saving with ToD tariffs are contradicted by subsidising electricity consumption in the agricultural sector. Therefore, changes of the tariff system are required in terms of optimised electricity saving incentives.

The tasks of the background study and the stakeholder analysis are, first, to monitor efficiency issues in the energy sector and, second, to analyse governance structures in the electricity sector, e.g. utility regulation, and preferences of stakeholders, individuals, and interest groups. These modules provide the building blocks for the reference scenario for the energy sector of Hyderabad and the regulatory framework of Andhra Pradesh. The scenario is required to identify needs and capacities for low emission energy generation, minimised T & D losses, and energy efficient consumption patterns. These data indicate demand for institutional changes for the implementation of efficiency enhancements. With the data of the background study we will derive the institutional changes and capacity building required for the adaptation of energy efficient technologies and the strategies to that effect that are to be pursued in the demonstration projects. The demonstration projects will form the outcome of the background study and the stakeholder analysis. The stakeholders in co-operation with Indian and German firms will implement the identified efficiency improvements according to the needs and capacities of the end users. The results of demonstration projects, such as decentralised technologies for cooking and lighting, electricity saving measures, particularly for irrigation in the agricultural sector, and promotion of green electricity, will be used for further modelling of the efficiency scenario and provide input for the "Sustainable Development Framework" and the "Perspective Action Plan". The analytical part of the background study is closely interlinked with the activities of the Work Packages 2.1, 3.2. B, and 3.2. C.This networking ensures full consideration of all criteria for mitigation and adaptation strategies in terms of energy efficiency improvements. The following modules give a summary of the entire process up until milestone two:

Efficiency monitoring

1. The first part of the background study localises and quantifies energy efficiency failures, such as insufficient economic incentives for efficient energy technologies, high mitigation and administration costs, as well as emissions, knowledge deficits, and import dependencies. With these data the background study provides a basis for efficiency monitoring in terms of examining the determinants of inefficient production and consumption patterns.

2. Together with the results of the stakeholder analysis, efficiency monitoring determines measures and activities of stakeholders to develop appropriate strategies for establishing energy saving technologies and supporting efficient behaviour on part of firms and consumers.

3. Regulatory models applied by the APERC require further optimisation in terms of exploiting all options for setting incentives to energy efficiency behaviour. For example, open access charges reduces attractiveness of open access significantly.

4. Power cuts strictly restrict firms in expanding their output level. Mainly small-scale firms suffer from this restriction due to very limited investment capital and insufficient supply of micro-credits.

5. Establishment of low cost measures for energy savings requires detailed knowledge of consumer behaviour and willingness to pay for improvements according to power purchase parity.

Further steps of the background study

1. The second part of the background study builds upon the results of the first part of the background study, involves the network approach of the stakeholder analysis and calculates efficiency gains in all fields of the energy sector. This continues the

previous inter-action with activities of other Work Packages, particularly WP 2.1, 3.2. B, 3.2. C and 4:

   a) further examination of power generation, transmission and distribution regarding effects on energy supply and security in Hyderabad. Installed capacity in Andhra Pradesh has increased by 25 % between 2007 and early 2009. Actual data on the distribution of this additional capacity to the DISCOM are not available, hence data acquisition will be part of the empirical analysis until milestone two,

   b) analysis of energy market regulation, and price developments with regards to purchasing power parity,

   c) analysis of investment behaviour of public and private energy utilities using expert interviews. Additional interviewing that picks up on the interviews already conducted in the initial phase of the Work Package 3.2 A,

   d) analysis of commercial energy consumption employing expert interviews in the business sector,

   e) specific emphasis on the needs of small-scale firms and cooperatives,

   f) efficiency analysis of consumer behaviour utilising the CVM and choice experiments based on new developments and own experiences,

   g) analysis of rural-urban linkages in the energy sector regarding cross-relations of efficiency measures,

   h) calculation of marginal mitigation cost curves for households and firms.

2. The background study for the first milestone provides the data background for the analytical section of the background study, which is to be completed by the second milestone, and for further modelling of the efficiency analysis as part of the scenario process at the centre of the entire project. Moreover, the entire background study provides data for cost benefit analysis of mitigation strategies and policies, such as energy saving technologies.

3. Fields of application for demonstration projects in the energy sector will be prepared by milestone one. The stakeholder analysis identifies stakeholders´ capacities and interest in demonstration projects. Co-operation with stakeholders, such as ECM and Osmania University of Hyderabad, for the development of demonstration projects has been initialised so far in the fields of renewable energy use for cooking, fuel substitution with biomass for cars and motorcycles, combination of CDM measures by German industry with efficiency improvements through sub-

stitution of lamps for energy saving lamps (first targets are Osram and Bosch). Further activities will deal with drivers of and obstacles to sustainable applications. Moreover, financing programs will be developed in co-operation with stakeholders and investors by milestone two. Preparation of workshops, for example in co-operation with the BDI with both sets of actors has already been started in the period leading up to milestone one.

4. By September 2009, TERI will deliver data on price developments in the energy sector in Hyderabad with special attention paid to economic effects on households, firms, and the public sector. The analysis of these price developments is part of the reference scenario to be finalised by milestone two.

5. Until milestone two in September 2010 the total background study of Work Package 3.2. A provides background for the deliverables of Work Package 5 and contributes to the concept study which is subject to this deliverable. The concept study will provide pathways of development for demonstration projects and government structures based on the descriptive and analytical output of the background study.

References

APCPDCL (Andhra Pradesh Central Power Distribution Company Ltd.). 2007. Tariff Order on Retail Supply Business for the FY 2007-08 of APCPDCL, APNPDCL, APSPDCL and APEPDCL.

APCPDCL. 2008. www.apcentralpower.com/content/APCPDCL/View3.2.1.jsp.

APERC (Andhra Pradesh Central Power Distribution Company Ltd.). 2009. www.ercap.org/.

APTRANSCO (Andhra Pradesh Transmission Corporation and Distribution Companies). 2007. "Administration Report 2006-2007", 9th Administration Report, Hyderabad.

Bollino, C.A. 2009. "The Willingness to Pay for Renewable Energy Sources: The Case of Italy with Socio-demographic Determinants." *The Energy Journal* 30(2):81–96.

Deambi, S. (ed.). 2008. *From Sunlight to Electricity. A practical handbook on solar photovoltaic applications*. Revised Edition, TERI Press, New Delhi.

GoAP (Government of Andhra Pradesh). 2007. Statistic Abstract.

GoAP. 2003. The Electricity Act.

Grigsby, L.L. et al. 2001. *The Electric Power Engineering Handbook*. USA: CRC Press.

Grösche, P. and C. Vance. 2009. "Willingness to Pay for Energy Conservation and Free-Ridership on Subsidization: Evidence from Germany." *The Energy Journal* 30(2): 135–153.

Indiastat. 2009. www.indiastat.com.

Infraline India. 2009. www.infraline.com.

Koteswara, M. R. and L. M. Krishna. 2007. "Power transmission development in Andhra Pradesh." *Indian Journal of Power and River Valley Development* 58(5/6): 76–79.

Lamb, P. 2006. *The Indian Electricity Market: Country Study and Investment Context, Program on Energy and Sustainable Development*. Working Paper No. 48, Stanford University, Stanford.

Morrison, M. and C. Nalder. 2009. "Willingness to Pay for Improved Quality of Electricity Supply Across Business Type and Location." *The Energy Journal* 30(2): 117–133.

Pal, S. 2008. "Best practices and innovation in tariff regulation in electricity sector." In *Regulatory Performance in India.* edited by S.K. Sarkar, V. Aggarwal, S. Malik and R. Chawla: 180–184. The Energy and Resources Institute (TERI), New Delhi.

Rommel, K. and J. Meyerhoff. 2009. "Empirische Analyse des Wechselverhaltens von Stromkunden. Was hält Stromkunden davon ab, zu Ökostromanbietern zu wechseln?" *Zeitschrift für Energiewirtschaft* 33(1): 74–82.

Rommel, K. and J. Meyerhoff. 2007." Are Cost Based Green Power Promotion Schemes Efficient? A Comparison of Feed-in Tariffs and Consumer Preferences." In *Competition Policy in Network Industries* edited by F. Fichert, J. Haucap, J. and K. Rommel: 179–202. LIT-Verlag, Vol. 3, Berlin.

Rommel, K. 2006. "Willingness To Pay for Green Power and Implications for Energy Policy in Japan." *Journal of Environmental Economics* 17(2): 1–16.

Sakar, S. K., V. Aggarwal, S. Malik and R. Chawla. 2008. *Regulatory Performance in India. Achievements, constrains, and future action.* TERI Press, New Delhi.

Sant, G. 2008. "Consumer involvement in the regulatory process: power sector." edited by S.K. Sarkar, V. Aggarwal, S. Malik and R. Chawla: 227–232. The Energy and Resources Institute (TERI), New Delhi.

Sarkar, S. K., K. Deb and M. Sundararaman. 2002. *Reforms in the infrastructure sectors: next steps.* TERI Press, New Delhi.

Shukla, P. R., D. Biswas, T. Nag, A. Yajnik, T. Heller and D.G. Victor. 2004. *Impact of Power Sector Reforms on Technology, Efficiency and Emissions: Case Study of Andhra Pradesh, India.* PESD Working Paper No. 20.

Shukla, P. R., S. Dhar and D. Mahapatra. 2008. "Low-carbon society scenarios for India." *Climate Policy* 8: 156–176.

TERI. 2007. *Regulation in practice in the Indian electricity sector: Analysis of distribution tariff orders.* TERI Press, New Delhi.

United Nations Population Division. 2001. *World Urbanization Prospects: The 2001 Revision.* UN Publications, New York.

United States Green Building Council. 2006. *Foundations of the Leadership in Energy and Environmental Design, Environmental Rating System: A Tool for Market Transformation.*

United States Green Building Council. 2009. *Green Building Facts.*

Appendix

A.1 Power plants operated by APGENCO

APGENCO	MW	Type
Vijayawada Thermal Power Station	1,760	thermal
Rayalaseema Thermal Power Project	840	thermal
Kothagudem Thermal Power Station V Stage	500	thermal
Kothagudem Thermal Power Station	700	thermal
Ramagundam 'B" Thermal Power Station	62.5	thermal
Tungabhadra/Hampi Power House	57.8	hydel
Priyadarshini Jurala HEP	78	hydel
Penna Ahobilam HES	20	hydel
Mini Hydro power stations	10.6	hydel
Singur HES	15	hydel
Nizamsagar HES	10	hydel
Pochampad HES	27	hydel
Donkarayi Canal Power House	25	hydel
Machkund HES	84	hydel
Upper Sileru HES	240	hydel
Lower Sileru HES	460	hydel
Nagarjunasagar HES	815.6	hydel
Nagarjunasagar Right Canal Power House	90	hydel
Nagarjunasagar Left Canal Power House	60	hydel
Srisailam Left Bank Power House	900	hydel
Srisailam Right Bank Power House	770	hydel
Ramgiri Wind Farm	2	wind
Total	**7527.5**	

Source: www.apgenco.gov.in, 2009

A.2 Central and private power generation in Andhra Pradesh

Company	Name	MW	Fuel
Gas (Joint-Venture)			
APGPCL	Vijjeswaram	272	gas
Public (without APGENCO)			
NTPC	Ramagundam	2,600	coal
NTPC	Simhadri	1,000	coal
IPPs			
Reliance (BSES)	Samalkot	220	gas
Lanco Group (+Genting)	Kondapalli (Stage 1)	368	gas
Lanco Group (+Genting)	Kondapalli (Stage 2)	368	gas
GVK	Jegurupadu I	216	gas
GVK	Jegurupadu II	220	gas

Company	Name	MW	Fuel
GVK	Gauthami	464	gas
GMR Group	Vemagiri	388.5	gas
Spectrum Power Generation	Kakinada	208	gas
Konaseema Gas Power LTD	Konaseema	460	gas
Private demand			
Essar Power	Visakhapatnam	25	coal
Vizag Steel	Visakhapatnam	236	coal

Source: www.apind.gov.in/whyap1.html

A.3 Power consumption 2007-08 in Hyderabad (LT)

Category	MU
LT I Domestic	1733.28
LT II Non-Domestic	794.68
LT II + IV Industry	188.78
LT V Agriculture	0
LT VI + VII + VIII	106.54
Total	**2,823.28**

Source: www.apdes.ap.gov.in/AP%20admin%20Setup.htm

A.4 Services connected in Hyderabad (as on March 31, 2007)

Category	Nos. of services
LT I Domestic	1,012,992
LT II Non-Domestic	209,555
LT III Industrial	13,187
LT IV Cottage Industry and Dhobi Ghats	40
LT V Agricultural (including RESCOs)	1,003
LT VI Public Lighting	7,295
LT VII General Purpose	4,898
LT VIII Temporary	10
Total LT	1,248,980
Total HT	1,072
LT + HT	**1,250,052**

Source: APTransco Administration Report 2005-07: 128

A.5 Installed capacity in Andhra Pradesh

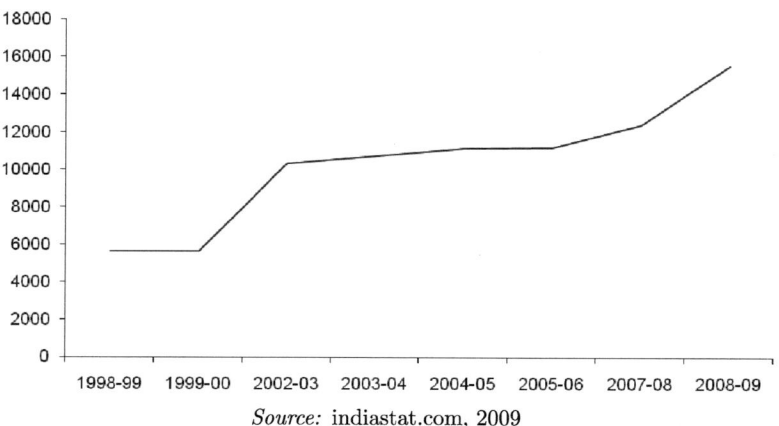

Source: indiastat.com, 2009